Light FROM the Darkness:
A Different Perspective on
Difficult Times

Light FROM the Darkness: A Different Persective on Difficult Times

BY CHANA KLEIN

ISBN-10 069261933X
ISBN-13 9780692619339

Cover Design by Manaaraa Art in Sri Lanka
Illustration Artists: Cintia Sand, Richie Williams, and Rukmali Fernando
Author Photograph by Heshie Klein, MD

Published by
Light FROM the Darkness Creations
New Jersey
2016

For information contact
chana@lightfromthedarkness.com

TABLE OF

CONTENTS

FORWARD

By Rabbi Simcha Weinberg, Shlita

TM
The Foundation Stone

This wise book by Chana Klein will guide you in finding your Light and in using it to rise from the Darkness.

It was clear from the moment I met Chana that she was a Light in the Darkness, but little did I appreciate how powerful a Light.

Her sunny personality, the way she greets everyone she meets, her insights into the text, and her ability to reframe challenging issues all contribute to appreciating her Light. But there is so much more.

I've had the ability to observe her overcome one challenge after another; problems that would crush most people, and her spirit shines more powerfully as she lives her approach of Light from the Darkness. Her Light increases while confronted with Darkness. But there is still more.

I learned from Chana that I have my own Darkness and she inspired me to find my Light. Chana shares her Light, and when experiencing her Light we appreciate her Light in the Darkness in a new way. Yet, there is more.

People enter her office, begin a phone session with her, enveloped in pain, confusion, illness, "conditions," Darkness. They finish their sessions filled with her Light. Chana is not only able to find Light in her life, she turns on the Light in other people stuck in their own Darkness.

Chana now shares her Light with her stories. The Darkness she battled is real. Her Light is even more so.

May God bless her with joy, love, success, and even more Light she can share with the world.

Sincerely,

Rabbi Simcha L. Weinberg
President

ACKNOWLEGEMENTS

Thank you to Rabbi Simcha Weinberg, Shlita, for 22 years of endless hours of deep, amazing, learning that remained new no matter how many years of learning took place.

Thank you Rabbi Menachem Meier, Shlita, for reading my manuscript, and reviewing and commenting to make it better and most for your support and enthusiasm for my work and my learning.

Thank you to my ex husband and friend, Heshie Klein, MD for your many hours of reviewing my manuscript and for your suggestions, many of which I did not follow but still appreciate the care and attention to every detail.

Thank you also for being the best photographer ever, shown on cover photo, proving it is the photographer and not the camera that takes a photo that gets to the essence of a person.

Thank you to the following wonderful artists: to Manaaraa_Art, Sri Lanka, the book cover artist, to Cintia Sand, who did the majority of the drawings of me as a child, to Richie Williams, and to Rukmali Fernando for your beautiful artwork at such reasonable prices.

Thank you to all of the brilliant women and men with whom I learn Torah everyday, too many to list. And Thank you also to the many rabbis whom I have been so blessed to listen to as well.

Thank you to God for rearranging my whole life with what seemed to be disasters that left me with time to work on my manuscripts and forced me to clear my body and my brain of all toxic substances and thoughts. Each disaster, for example, my roof caving in and flooding my whole house, making it impossible for me to see clients, turned out to be a Light From the Darkness.

INTRODUCTION

One who looks straight into the deepest darkness finds the most radiant light.

THE DARKEST PART

I look in the mirror.
I marvel at how my body has more systems and parts than I could list.

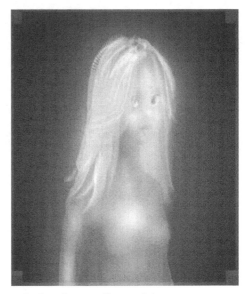

I notice the various colors and shades reflected in my image.

And then, it strikes me.

Only one part of my body is actually the
color black, the color of darkness.

That part is the pupil of my eye.

It strikes me as very strange.

That the pupil of the eye is the part of

the body into which light enters.

And the white of the eye, that appears

to be light, cannot see any light.

That means that the only part of the

body through which light can enter is

the darkest part.

The light that I see comes in through the

pupil,

the blackest, darkest spot on my body.

In the same way, light comes from the

darkness.

So it has been for me . . .

THE DARKEST SPOT: AN

ALLEGORICAL STORY

It is a time of war.

A young man is taken captive.

His captors do not kill him right away.

They, instead, give him an opportunity

to save his own life.

A dark hood is placed over his head to

cover his eyes.

Then, they bring him to the opening of a

deep cave.

They untie his hands and feet and shove

him in.

"You have four days," one of them barks.

"You will either find your way out of here, and be free . . . or you will die of starvation."

He hears their footsteps fade in the distance.

The young man rips off the hood.

He finds himself alone in the dark.

His mind races to devise a way out of this cave.

His eyes dart from one edge to the other, from floor to ceiling.

There, he spots a slight flicker of light coming in from a spot on the curved roof of the cave.

"If I can get to that tiny spark of light,"
he figures. "I'll be able to find the way
out of here."

He jumps as high as he could, trying to
reach the light.

Next, he tries climbing the walls of the
cave.

He searches for something to raise him
up higher to reach that spot of light.

He piles up dirt, and then piles up
rocks, all in an effort to get closer to the
light.

He works and works, to the point of
exhaustion.

To no avail . . .

By the end of the 4th day in the cave, the
young man dies.

On the 5th day, one of the captors comes
to collect the body.

With one hand, the captor pushes aside
a large rock that is lodged in the darkest
spot on the bottom of the cave.

Pushing that rock opens the cave . . .

Bringing light into it.

From the darkest spot!

The real way out of the cave was to be
found in the darkest spot of the abysmal
cave.

The young man had searched for the
answer only where he could see some
light.

He had not even thought of the fact that

his life could have been saved by going

to the darkest spot in the cave, the spot

that had no apparent light at all.

How often have the answers appeared

from the darkness itself?

How often have we found that when we

face the darkness, it becomes light?

The prophet tells us:

"I will give you treasure concealed in the

dark."

(Isaiah 45:3)

Just as yin becomes yang, the darkness

becomes light.

That greatest light can be found in the darkest spot.

And so it was with me.

My story is not about light IN the darkness.

Rather it is about light FROM the darkness.

It is about the darkest events, the darkest times, and about finding light from that darkness.

PERSPECTIVE

My eyes have viewed all of which I am about to tell. It is all my subjective experience.

I imagine that those with whom I have interacted will likely have their own version and explanation.

People believe what they choose to believe.

They see what they want to see.

I imagine that if the people about whom I write were to tell this story it would be from a totally different point of view.

IT COULD NEVER HAPPEN???

In high school creative writing class, the teacher assigned us the writing of

a short story.

I couldn't think of what to write.

So I wrote things that were happening

in my own life.

I named the main character Vera (after

my best friend, Veeta).

The day after I handed it in, the teacher

called me to her desk.

She asked me to read my story to the class.

There, I stood in front of the room, raw, before all of them.

I was sure they would know that the story was really my story, the story of what was happening in my life.

The students listened attentively.

Once I finished, the teacher asked for the students' comments:

"It's a good story!"

They all nodded.

Then one said after the other:

"But it could never happen."

And another:

"It's not realistic."

All of the students agreed that it is a good story; but it could never happen. My peers did not want to see that one of their classmates had such a life.

So they said to each other, and to themselves, that it could never happen.

"It's no wonder that truth is stranger than fiction. Fiction has to make sense." Mark Twain

PEOPLE SEE WHAT THEY
BELIEVE

People don't believe what they see. Seeing something does not make them believe it is true.

Rather, people see what they believe.

They see what they already believe is true and often what they wish to be true, as in the case of my peers in high school.

Perception cannot be argued with.

"It is easier to fool people than to convince them that they have been fooled."   Mark Twain

While it is difficult for me to understand the way people in my life acted, I must trust that their own experiences and judgments led them to making their choices.

Perhaps the way they saw things made them do what they did.

"There are two ways to be fooled.

One is to believe what isn't true; the other is to refuse to believe what is true."   Søren Kierkegaard

DARKNESS AS A CREATION
BEFORE LIGHT

The Torah tells us that Darkness was created before Light was created.

The world was created in darkness . . . and God said Let there be light . . . (Genesis 1:1-3)

Each special day on the Jewish calendar begins at nightfall.

Each day begins when it is dark.

Darkness is not merely the absence of light.

According to the blessings before the Jewish prayer known as the Shema, Darkness is a separate creation.

The Blessings of the Shema prayer state that God "forms light and creates darkness." Isaiah 45:7

" *'Let there be Lights from the Darkness,'*
He declared – and so it was!" Yom Kippur Machzor: Blessings of the Shema p. 327

I write what I experienced.

I write from my own perspective.

I write what happened in my life.

And most important. . . I write how I found light from the darkness that had been enveloping me.

HAUNTED

It was my first Shabbos in Brooklyn. As I walked in the street that Shabbos afternoon, I was haunted in my mind's eye by screams of children coming from behind front doors of houses.

With that image came a sickening awareness that no one cares.

I didn't know where this overpowering image was coming from. But it felt so real.

After Shabbos, I inquired about a local

food place.

That is when I found out that the

neighborhood where I was walking and

hearing the screams is a few blocks from

where I resided as a child.

I was there without realizing its

location.

The darkness of the beatings hit me, of

the screams, the neglect, the rejections.

The feelings of affliction, were literally

haunting me.

The power of such darkness was in the

air, in the neighborhood, in my body,

and in my spirit.

Powerless over the flashbacks, I decided
to look the darkness in the eye.

That night, I visited each place that was
haunting me: PS 98, Dr. Brandstein's
office, 3128 Kings Highway where I
lived with my parents and brother,
Eleanor, my childhood friend's house.

I physically showed up at each place
where a dark horror happened.

I talked to each place staring straight
into it.

Through my terror, I was facing each
darkness.

As I persisted, the only thing that
prevailed within me was a vision and a
feeling of Light.

The Light that came to me From the
Darkness.

THE DARKNESS IN THE

BEGINNING

T he world began with Darkness.
So too, did my life.

I am considered, by those who know
me, to be a passionately happy person,
always with a warm, jubilant smile,
resonating bubbling energy.

I have been told that I am a loving
person and that my smile lights up the
stage, that my energy lights up a room,
that my presence lights up the lives of
others.

In my late 60's, I am voted "The Most
Energetic Player" by the trainers and
participants at a conference of 300
people where the average age was about
35 years old.

It comes from deep inside me.

It's real.

But first I tell my beginning.

This was The Darkness...

From the Darkness came my Light.

SCENES FROM MY EYES AS A CHILD

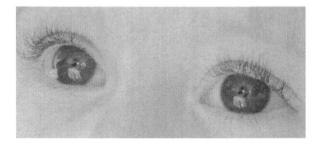

ZAYDIE

I am not yet two years old. Zaydie (Grandpa in Yiddish) loves me. He plays with me.

Even though he scares me with his play, like when he dresses as a ghost, he is the attention that I get.

Then, no more Zaydie . . . No one ever explains where he is. Not a word is said.

I find out, when I'm an adult, that Mommy and Daddy moved out of the apartment while Zaydie was praying in the synagogue on Shabbos (the Sabbath) morning.

He returned to the apartment expecting Shabbos lunch.

The apartment was locked and the furniture moved out.

No one mentioned his name to me ever again.

No one explained to me that I will never again see my Zaydie.

But I always remember him.

Years later, when I am 48 years old, my brother, Michael, passes to the next world.

At the gravesite, I see Zaydie's grave, near Michael's.

The stone reads: "Aron Gordon – Died October 19, 1955 - Age 82 Years - Avinu HaYikar (our beloved father)."

That was Zaydie.

Apparently, he lived until I was ten years old.

I realize that Zaydie had been alive all that time!!!

I throw myself on the ground near the
grave and cry bitter tears.
I cry because he had been there and I
did not know.
Oh, how I missed out.
Oh, how we both lost out.

That I could have had one person tell
me what to do, and tell me what a Torah
is, and all about God.
Oh, that I could have had my Zaydie!
Oh, the loss we both had.

But in the 1980's, when I took on the
commandment of not driving on
Shabbos, I walked five miles to shul
(synagogue) each Shabbos.

I felt Zaydie with me, the whole 2½

hour walk, watching from his resting

place.

I felt his smile and satisfaction at my

Shabbos observance.

For one whole year, it never rained or

snowed on my walk.

SANDWICH

I'm at the table with Mommy, Daddy, and Michael.

The waiter serves me a cold cuts deli sandwich. It tastes really good.

I want to make sure I have it for another time.

So I save the other half for later. I wrap it into a napkin.

I place it in my little purse and snap it closed.

The following Saturday, in my bedroom, I take out my purse from my closet shelf.

Anticipating the other half of the delicious sandwich, I unfold the napkin, into which I had placed it.

There it is, in the same folded napkin.

But I'm confused.

It stinks.

It smells like a bowel movement.

I don't understand what could have happened to it.

Did someone find it and replace it with
something else?

This is not what I had put into my
purse.

No one had ever told me that food can
spoil.

LOVING ANYWAY

I am three-and-a-half years old.
Mommy is home from the hospital.

Mommy's big fat belly has shrunk.

It's bedtime. I want to see the baby. I

want to meet my new brother.

I leave my bedroom and go to where I

hear a baby.

I open the door a crack and peek into

the room to see my new brother.

Mommy slams my head in the doorway.

Perhaps as I grew up, a part of me always hated a part of Michael, for I was clobbered for wanting to love him.

But as clobbered as I was, I never did stop loving.
No matter how my mother hurt me and suppressed me, she never did squelch my ability to love.

As much as she prohibited Michael from seeing me after she had left me, he eventually stopped obeying her despise for me and in the end we had a great brother-sister love.

PAJAMA PARTY

I am sooo excited. Mommy told me that I'm going to a pajama party. I have never before been to a pajama party. But I picture in my head how other five-year-old children will be there and how we will have cake and ice cream and play games in our pajamas. I'm so looking forward to the party in a way that only a child could.

The night before the party Grandma is
sleeping over.

I can hardly sleep because of my
excitement.

Grandma stays with me in bed early in
the morning.

I feel so happy that I'm going to a party
TODAY!

When it's time, Mommy and I, in my
pajamas, travel to a very large shiny
grey building.

It takes up the whole block and is very
high into the sky. We walk up a lot of
very wide steps in front of the building.

We enter through the wide doorways on
top of the high steps.

Inside, it is huge, with shiny floors and

counters along both side-walls.

I feel confused.

Where is the pajama party?

Where are the other children?

No one else I see is wearing their

pajamas.

We walk further into the large building.

Several adults are approaching me.

They're wearing white coats.

They're moving directly toward me.

They grab me.

I'm very confused and terrified.

I don't know them.

I kick and wave my arms.

I'm fighting for my life.

They're overpowering me.

They tie me down to a bed on wheels.

I'm crying.

No one cares.

They wheel me into a room.

They take off my pajamas . . . the

pajamas I was wearing to go to a party!

They put me on a hard cold table that is

as big as a bed.

I want to scream.

My mouth opens.

I have no voice.

They put a mask on my mouth.

The smell is awful.

I remember it always.

I feel I am dying, as I lose strength, and

then consciousness.

They're murdering me.

I am gone... consciousness lost.

And Mommy said I was going to a

pajama party.

Later, I wake up in a hospital bed that is

against a wall.

My throat hurts real bad.

I'm totally pissed. No way to express it.

Bad Mommy!

There was no party.

Instead, my tonsils were removed.

That memory gets buried into a slew of

other memories as I'm growing up . . .

Until, as a young adult, an oral surgeon

tries to fit me for an anesthesia mask. He

puts the mask over my mouth.

I run out of the chair in a panic.

I feel like he is trying to murder me.

Suddenly, I'm 5 years old again,

fighting off the doctors.

CAMP

It's a hot summer day.
The other campers give me the
nickname "Princess." That feels so good.
It means to me that they think I am
pretty.

I'm sitting alone in the woods behind
the sleeping quarters.
My butt is on the grass among the
dandelions and the ants.
The trees, so beautiful, hide my
presence on this spot.

I see a large refrigerator plugged into an
outlet. There are cartons of small milk
containers piled high, likely, awaiting
someone to put them away.

I open a container and drink the milk.

Then, another, and another, and
another.

I say to myself that if I drink a lot, then

it will be a very long time before I feel

the hunger that often accompanies me.

My belly hurts so bad from the fullness.

I could hardly move.

A few days later, I am hungry again.

It didn't work.

OH, THE SHAME THIS MOTHER HAS BROUGHT ME!

I'm a little girl in the house.
As I step out of the shower, my arm knocks the bottle of liquid soap onto the floor.

Uh oh, I spilled the soap!

Mommy sees.

Her face grimaces.

Her protruding, folded-back, orange tongue is held tight between her teeth.

A signal for me that a beating is

imminent.

I run out of the house . . . Naked.

My terror of her is stronger than my

concern that all of the neighbors are

seeing me running around the block . . .

naked.

I run in panic.

She's chasing me.

I keep running and running.

I turn the corner on the block.

She's close behind.

Two more blocks . . . out of breath...

I look back.

She's not in sight.

Now, I have to walk back to the house with all of the neighbors, sitting on their porches, looking at my naked body.

Oh, the shame.
Oh, the shame this mother has brought me.

SHAME ON THE TRAIN

We are on the train together,
coming home from an eye
doctor. I need surgery.

My mother appears very upset. I see her
tension.

We sit on the train.

There is a man sitting across from us.

My mother is eyeing him and he is
returning the attention.

She moves next to him and is squirming

excitedly near the strange man.

He responds by moving closer to her.

The next thing I see is that her hand

slaps his face.

He does not hit her back.

I feel such shame, such disdain.

I want so much to have someone to look

up to.

"In Thee I have trusted, let me not be

ashamed." Psalm 25

"MEN WILL HURT YOU!"

"Men will hurt you!" she tells me.

Even as a young child, I could see the hurt and the hardness in my mother.

It frightens me.

I think about what will be in my life.

She says men will hurt me.

But I feel as if there would be no other option than to be hurt.

She says it often - how men will hurt
me.

I don't understand.

Who I am, could not take it in.

Compared to my desperate need for
human interaction, the fear of getting
hurt seems minuscule.

So, instead of dreading being hurt . . .

I yearn to be loved, held, and respected.

No matter how many times I am hurt
and no matter how deeply. . .

I choose to love others as if I had never
been hurt.

To love and to be there for another
person becomes my greatest fulfillment.

As a child, I'm comforted by fantasies of being saved by some cowboy and going out into the wilderness with him to survive.

SNEER

My father wears a perennial sneer.

God gave him a handsome face

and a good build.

He hardly ever talks.

I'm terrified of him.

Neither he, nor my mother, is

predictable.

I never really know when the next

beating is going to come down on me.

Or even worse . . . when I'm going to be left alone in the house for endless periods of time.

The beatings were welcomed when compared to the all-alone times.

HAPPY BIRTHDAY???

My winter coat has become too short and too tight. My father works in the garment industry with access to lots of clothes that he often brings to the house.

I ask him for a coat because this one is too small.

He tells me I will get one on my

birthday.

I continue to wear the tight coat

anticipating my birthday to get a new

one.

My birthday is finally here.

But no mention of a coat.

I remind Daddy that he promised me a

new coat.

I get a bad beating.

But this one is as if it has a wise lesson

he thinks that he is teaching me.

That is that I should have known not to

ask him, he tells me.

For the rest of my life I keep my

birthday a secret.

I hear friends celebrating their birthdays

with others.

I remember mine, spent alone, because

it is the only way I can handle it even in

my older years.

I never mention my birthday to anyone.

It comes. It passes.

The day ends and I am still here.

My birthday is the darkest darkness of

all as I am growing up.

As the years go on, it is less dark.

The darkness is because it is supposed

to be a happy day.

Days that are supposed to be happy are

the saddest ones of all.

MIRROR, MIRROR

Mommy is standing in front of the
full-length mirror of the closet
door opposite my room.
She's flashing her left hand fingers in
the air, admiring the shiny red ring on
her finger.

"Somebody loves me! Somebody loves
me!" she is loudly exclaiming, again and
again, as she strokes her nude body
with her right hand going up and down,

making a path from above her right

breast down to her thighs.

Daddy is pacing back and forth.

He is sneering, a quiet rage.

He slams into their bedroom, which is

next to mine.

In one swoop of the arm, he heaves

everything from her dressing bureau (all

the things that make her pretty) onto the

floor.

Michael and I stand in the middle of

this, unnoticed.

VIGILS

The fights are loud. I hear them in the next room.
I stay awake listening until the wee hours of the morning, as if on a vigil to stop one from murdering the other.

I fear waking up to find one of them full of blood . . . and dead.

Somehow, I sense, that if I stay awake all night, I can prevent the murder.

I listen intently, alone and terrified . . .
until it gets quiet.

Then, I drift off into sleep.

DO I LOVE YOU?

I need to love and to be loved.
I'm a human being.
We all need love.
There is no-one, other than my mother,
from whom to get love.
But she is inconsistent.

There are times when she makes me feel
she loves me.
Many nights she comes in my room,
when she thinks I'm sleeping and asks

the "sleeping" me, "Do you believe I love you?"

I imagine that she thinks that I would say my true feelings if I am asleep.

But I'm really not asleep.

I answer, "No!"

She walks out.

Her just asking me what I think makes me feel that she in some way cares. It makes me feel that she cares what I believe and that she wants me to think she loves me.

Looking back, as an adult, I think she felt guilty for rejecting me. So at night, when I was supposedly sleeping, she would try to alleviate those guilt feelings by hearing me say that I felt loved.

Somehow she knew that I needed to feel loved.
And she knew that she did not give me that love.

THE TULIPS

I'm eight years old and I see beautiful,
tall tulips growing on the side of a

house on our block.

I don't realize that they are the pride of

the woman who planted them.

I have zero awareness of the fact that

they belong to anyone but God.

I marvel at how pretty they are.

So, I pluck them.

I give them to my mother to show her I

love her . . .

And probably to get her to love me.

I go to my room.

I am playing with my crayons.

Each crayon is a different color with a
different shaped head and so in my
imagination each has a different
personality.

I arrange my blanket on my bed as if it
were a village with peaks and valleys
and crevices in which the crayon
characters live.

The crayons have a voice and converse
with each other in my make-believe
world.

As I play the drama of the crayons, both
my mother and father barge into my
room.

Their anger is great.

They beat me, and beat me, and beat
me.

They say. . . because I picked the
flowers.

I didn't know that it was wrong.

I had no idea.

No one ever explained.

As an adult, I look back and feel so
badly for the lady whose flowers I took.

But as a child, how could I know that?

EVERYONE HEARS

When I'm beaten, I scrunch up my body.

My arms are over my face.

My knees are folded against my

stomach.

Trying to prevent the blows from

hurting me.

I'm screaming loud enough to make my

throat hurt.

Kicks, strap, fists, all at me.

Broken bones, bruises, strap marks on

my body wounded feelings.

Screams .   . . more screams.

All   of the

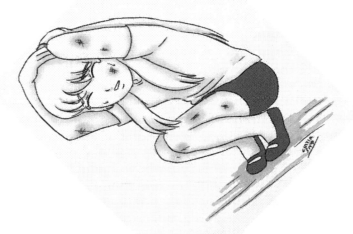

neighbors   hear.

They hear me   screaming.

Everyone knows. They all hear.

No one helps.

No one questions what is happening to

me, a little girl, in that house.

No one protects me.

People think it's none of their business.

Later, I go to Dr. Brandstein, whose

office is on the next block.

He tells me I need to see an orthopedic

doctor who can fix my broken bones.

No one takes me.

I hurt and eventually the pain is less.

LITTLE GIRL

It's hard to be present for the beatings
and it's harder to be present for the
neglect.
While I'm being hit, the well-adjusted
part of me leaves.
That is the part of me who always has a
smile.
Then, the "Little Girl" part of me has to
receive the whole beating.
That way, a part of me is able to go on
and function in the world.

BOTTOMLESS WELL: A
VISUALIZATION

The world of the Little Girl is a world of horror.

The Little Girl is visualized as an almost formless fetus falling down a bottomless well.

Her parents and brother are at the top of the well.

They are looking down at her. They laugh.

They're glad she is descending into the bottomless well.

They just go about their business with

no care or thought of the little girl.

Little Girl keeps falling deeper into the

well as her life at home is too grueling to

face.

The well stays with her . . . but she is not

aware of its presence.

Little Girl lives in the well for years to come, while the other part of her, the one who left during the beatings, functions in the world.

Eventually, as an adult, I speak to Little Girl everyday in my journal.
I don't know what I am feeling unless I write to Little Girl.
She writes back through my hand and tells me how she is doing.
I get to know her.

After many letters to Little Girl and years later, I unify Little Girl with the healthier part of me.
The healthier "me" apologizes to Little Girl for letting her take the beatings.

I promise her that from that day on, I
will be present for what happens.

I promise to take the abuse instead of
mentally leaving.

I write her that I will learn to deal with
it in a more present way.

As events seem to repeat themselves, I
begin to see that part of my road in life
is to learn to not allow myself to be
abused.

Part of my Life-Lessons was to be able
to be with all parts of myself, rather
than to walk away and go on as if it
didn't happen.

The only way I can learn the lessons that
my soul needs to learn is to be in the

situation which makes me cry out to learn each lesson so it stops happening to me.

How can I learn the soul lesson of how to fight abuse if I don't experience any?

SAVIOR OR EXECUTIONER?

My caretakers are also my executioners.

Swimming in the water, I feel Mommy

holding me under the water.

I can't breathe. I struggle.

She lets go.

I climb out of the water.

When I'm an adult, I tell my therapist

what happened.

He asks, "What did you do after that?"

I tell him "I went on with my day."

What else would I do?

Who would I run to?

Who would I cry to?

My mother?

Will I tell her a bad lady tried to hurt

me?

Would I confront her?

I was not even clear enough to know

how wrong she was.

It was probably too scary to face the real

truth.

That would mean that I'm truly alone.

Like the memory of Mommy choking

me as I lay in my crib, a memory that

reawakened with the panic that I felt

when my husband touched my neck.

When Mommy tries to hurt me, she is the one who also saves me.

It feels safer to look only at the savior mommy, and not at the bad mommy.

AFTER THE BEATING

The bad feeling after the beating.
No one acknowledges.

No one admits.

No one has a kind word.

No one to make it better.

No one sees who I really am.

Evil intentions are ascribed to me.

I am vilified, when I intend for only

loving good.

Then, I have to get up and go on

with the perennial knowledge that I am

not safe, even and especially, with those

who are supposed to make me safe and

keep me safe.

No one admitting what they did.

My forever being misjudged.

Accused of what I did not do.

Threatened with rejection, with

elimination, if I don't go along with

their lies.

People see what they want to believe.

And I have to go on whether I want to

or not.

Knowing that I have to do the right

thing, always.

That is all I have.

That is all I ever have, myself and my

choosing to do what I feel is right.

My integrity, my honesty, my

compassion for others.

That is all that is mine.

No one can take that away.

WATCHING

Walking home from school on Avenue Z, I watch children run into the arms of their daddy or mommy.

I see the joy, excitement, and anticipation of the great comfort they are about to receive.

Comfort that I never experienced.

Never someone to take care of things so that I may relax and trust.

With the pain, though, is the uninvited growth, the unavoidable connection with my Creator, and the lessons of how to take care of things with only His help and no one else's.

But when I see those children run into welcoming loving arms, I still cry for the child who I had been.

I cry for the child who had no arms into which to run.

NO-ONE HOME

I'm arriving home from school. I ring the doorbell. No one answers the door.

No one is home.

I'm outside the house, knocking on the door, and knocking, and knocking. Still, no one answers the door.

I need to go to the bathroom.

I continue to bang on the door.

I know it's futile.

Now, I'm banging on the door to release

energy ..

and to release yet another

disappointment.

I can't hold it in anymore.

I pee in my pants.

My blue and white sailor outfit is now

warm with my urine and quickly

becoming cooler.

SOMEONE BAD

Another day, the door is unlocked. But no one is home.

I'm scared that someone might be hiding in a closet, or someplace else in the house . . .

Someone bad.

I walk up the stairs.

My heart pounds as my breath stops.

I grab the door of each closet and swiftly pull it open, as I shout a loud sound to scare the invader, more than I'm scared myself.

No one is found.

I am alone.

I'm alone even after it has been dark for hours.

I'm so bored.

I bang my head on the back of the living room couch.

I cry from the loneliness.

No one is home.

STAYING OUT

When Mommy leaves for the
night, Daddy sneers more than
usual and spits. His movements are

agitated and abrupt.

This is the atmosphere that precedes a

beating.

It's familiar.

I have two choices – stay home and try

to sleep. . . .

but risk getting a bruising beating

- or - walk the streets and be accosted

by drunks.

I choose the latter.

I leave the house.

It's nighttime.

I wander around the streets of

Sheepshead Bay.

I walk and walk, my stomach churning .
. .

Too scared to go home.

I'm more afraid of going home and

being beaten by my father than I am of

the drunks who approach me on the

street.

I'm on-edge. I'm tired. I have no

awareness of what time it is.

I wonder how much longer before

school will begin for the day. I go to the

school building of PS 98 on Avenue Z
and East 26th Street.

It's still dark outside.

I sit on the wide step in front of the
main entrance door. I fall asleep.

A cop shines a light in my eyes, waking
me up from a light sleep.

"What are you doing here?"

"I'm afraid to go home. My father will
beat me."

"Go home!" he tells me.

In the 1950's, police do not get involved
in domestic violence.

There is no protection other than what I
create for myself.

I don't obey the officer.

I walk around the block and then return

to the step on which I resume my sleep.

I'm not yet aware that one washes in the

morning.

I go to school with the other children

when they arrive.

FAKER

I'm 10 years old. I get a beating.
As usual, I don't know that I did
anything bad.

Besides the strap marks and bruises,

sharp pain in my hip makes it hard to

walk. I'm limping. Mommy is saying

that I'm a faker

and that it doesn't really hurt.

Michael is agreeing with her that I

walked without

limping.

How they hate

me.

It hurts so much

to walk.

I try to bike

instead.

Mommy sees me

on the bike, as

she looks out the

window.

She says that

proves that I'm faking.

LEFT ALONE

Mommy leaves the house. Usually when Mommy leaves the house, Daddy beats me.

But this time I'm lucky. Daddy leaves also, but not with Mommy.

I'm home alone, so far, for a few days.

I try to go to the movies, to the Sheepshead Bay Theater, to see "The Creature from the Black Lagoon" with my friends.

We are walking the mile to the theater.

I'm walking slowly and laboriously

behind my friends, as I agonize each

step.

The pain doesn't allow me to keep up

with their pace.

They don't wait for me.

They're way ahead, out of sight.

Finally, I get to the theater.

I pay for my ticket .

I enter the theater and look for my

friends.

The pain is piercing, very bad, very,

very bad.

I open my eyes to a sea of kids' faces

leaning over the seats, staring at me.

I don't remember passing out.

I have no memory of how I got to be

lying flat on my back in the aisle of the

theater.

I believe that I am faking.

I believe my mother, and that is what

she told me.

Several men carry me into a roomy,

carpeted office.

They place me in a chair by a large

mahogany desk which is angled in the

corner of the room.

I tell myself that I'll keep pretending

that I'm hurt for a little while.

Then, I'll get up and go home.

The pain is excruciating.

But I'm convinced that my mother is
right. I'm faking!

The chair is so uncomfortable for me.
I can't find a painless position.
I decide that it's time to get up.
Enough pretending!
I try to move my butt from the seat of
the chair.
But I can't move.
My leg is jumping involuntarily, as if it
has a will of its own.
I don't understand what is happening.

I'm so confused. Why can't I move
myself?
Wasn't I faking?

The movie theater man, wearing a suit
jacket over a white shirt, moves the
phone in front of me.

He tells me to call my parents.
I don't know where either of them is,
and it does not occur to me that that is
odd.
I dial what I think is my grandmother's
phone number.
(She is senile and would not have been
able to do anything. But at the time,
there is really no one else I could think
of to call.)

I hear the ring of the phone in my ear.
A man's voice answers.
"Grandma?" I ask

He tells me I have the wrong number.

I dial again.

It's the man again.

I try again and it's him again.

More tries.

Then, a lady answers.

She tells me that I have the wrong

number.

I keep dialing the same number.

Finally, after several more attempts, the

lady asks me my name.

I tell her.

She knows me.

She tells me that she is Eleanor's mother

and that the man is Eleanor's father.

ELEANOR

Eleanor had been my best friend when I lived on Kings Highway in Brooklyn.

We were very close until the beginning of 4th grade.

Eleanor's mother would ask me if I ate that day, and then she would feed me.

In the middle of the school year, we moved away, to Sheepshead Bay.

I had not really kept in touch with
Eleanor.

But here I was, calling her number,
when I had never even known her
phone number.

I had thought I was calling the number
of my grandmother.

Eleanor and I had never spoken on the
phone, for in the late 1940's to early 50's
kids didn't really use the telephone,
unless it was an emergency.

At least I never did.

How did I end up calling that number?

SAVED BY THE "WRONG NUMBER"

When they hear me calling on the phone, Eleanor's parents ask me where I am.
I tell them I'm at the Sheepshead Bay Theater and that I seem to be hurt.

Both of them come to the theater.
They park in the back of the theater and the men carry me to the car and place me in the back seat.

Mr. and Mrs. Block drive me to the hospital, as I lay on the back seat. Every time they go over the slightest bump I feel unbearable pain.

BROOKLYN JEWISH HOSPITAL

I'm lying on a stretcher in Brooklyn
Jewish Hospital.

The stretcher is placed against a stone-
like wall outside an X-ray room.

They move me onto the X-ray table.

They lift my knees and separate them

for the X-ray.

Excruciating pain . . .

Unbearable! And Non-Stop Pain!

They tell me they're looking for my

mother.

Mrs. Block, Eleanor's mother, finds me a

good doctor.

But they need Mommy's signature for

permission to treat me, to do surgery.

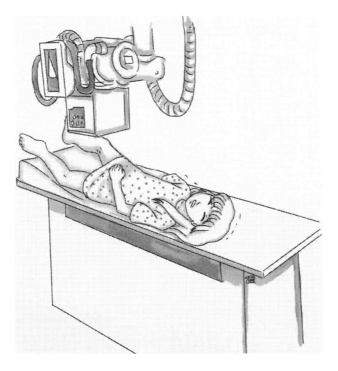

Lots of people ask me where Mommy

went. I don't know.

I tell them that they left a few days ago,

I tell them that they didn't tell me where

they are going.

I don't know when they're coming back.

During that whole night they are taking

me back to the X-ray machine very

often.

I find out later that they are seeing

"necrosis" from the hip down, which

means that my tissues are dying.

Necrosis cannot be treated.

It can only be removed.

The standard treatment is amputation of

the limb.

That is why they are taking X-rays so often.

I develop osteomyelitis and have to be in the hospital for about a year as the infection drains.

More X-rays, more excruciation!

I see through the opaque window next to my stretcher that it's dark outside.

Too much pain to sleep.

The night is very long.

It's light again and they still didn't find Mommy.

Another day on the stretcher,

More moving me onto the table for X-rays,

More unbearable pain!

THEY FOUND MOMMY

A nurse comes to my stretcher. She tells me the police found my mother.

I wait in anticipation of seeing her.

I wait a long time.

Finally, she walks up to the stretcher and tells me that the police found her, somehow, through our landlady whom she happened to call.

(Apparently, the police, in searching for my mother, had gotten in touch with our landlady who lived in the

apartment downstairs from us.)

The first thing I ask her is whether I will

miss my Girl Scout picnic next Sunday.

In all this, that was my biggest concern.

She tells me I'll have to miss it.

Missing the picnic was what I felt most

frustrated about.

I imagine that the rest was just too much

to feel.

It was decades until I let myself feel any

of it.

It's late at night.

But they wheel my stretcher to another

part of the hospital.

Dr. Jack Levine does surgery.

It can't wait until morning.

CAN'T TALK

I wake up.
I'm in a hospital bed next to a

window.

The sun glares through the window.

The room seems very bright . . .

Especially in comparison to the

darkness I feel within myself.

I open my eyes. I see a nurse.

Miss Harris is at the foot of my bed.

She talks to me cheerfully.

I don't answer her.

I can't talk.

I don't know why.

I can't move any part of my body, not even my lips.

For the remainder of the time that I stay in the hospital, Miss Harris often lovingly makes fun of me for not talking

at all during those first few days.

There were two nurses named Miss

Harris.

They were twins.

They were so good to me and made me

feel like they loved me.

They even invited me to their double-

wedding when they got married, many

months later.

I feel like I'm in a deep abyss.

More nurses come into the room.

Each one speaks to me.

I can't respond to any of them.

My body hurts.

It hurts a lot.

From the waist down, I can't move.

I don't understand what is happening.

I see my legs in casts.

The casts are connected with an iron bar

preventing me from moving.

There is a deep ache, and emptiness

inside me.

There's nothing I can do.

I'm powerless.

I can't play with my friends.

I can't move from the waist down.

I feel deep pain in my every fiber,

especially my spirit, and I don't

understand what is happening.

Where is my mother?

MY NEW HOME

I get a lot of attention from the staff in the hospital.

It becomes my home.

During painful procedures I ask the nurses to hold my hand.

They seem to understand and I feel they are there for me.

I get used to daily blood tests to the point where the needles that they stick in me don't bother me.

However, procedures like the
catheterization, in which they put a tube
up my urethra, is a burning torture.

I cry and beg them not to do that.

I even beg Dr. Levine to have them stop
doing that.

But they come back regularly to do it
again . . .

No matter how much I cry and tell them
it hurts.

No one ever explained to me why they
had to do that.

TICKLING TOES

D r. Levine comes every morning with a group of others in doctor coats.

He gives a talk to them about my condition, as they all look at me.

I smile at them and they smile at me.

They tickle my toes that stick out of the casts.

Each day doctors tickle my toes as they do their rounds.

But I'm unaware that my toes don't

move.

One morning, after being in my hospital

bed for about 6 months, my toes wiggle

upon being tickled.

Everyone around me gets excited and

joyous.

I don't even know that it's a concern

and so I'm just glad that they're happy.

I'm told that they had planned to

amputate my leg.

But they didn't because that night, my

mother wouldn't sign permission for

that.

She signed only for surgery.

I'm told they put my hip together with

screws and pins . . .

and that I will never be able to put any

weight on it.

Dr. Levine explains that he had to

remove 1/3 of my leg bone, making one

leg shorter than the other.

He says that the bone in my leg had lost

circulation.

I don't really know what that means and

never consider asking what the

connection is between walking and

circulation in my leg.

I don't even know what circulation is

and don't think to ask.

MOMMY'S MATZAH BREI

I can't eat.
I have no appetite.

I hear threats that they will feed me

intravenously again if I don't eat.

It doesn't make a difference.

I still can't eat.

When they ask me what I want to eat,

I tell them I want the matzah brei that

my mother makes during Passover.

That is the only food that I have an

appetite for.

It's the middle of the night.

I'm awake in my bed.

My room is right off the hall near the

elevator.

I hear the loud, clicking footsteps of a

woman's spiked heels coming from the

elevator.

I know it's my mother.

She's here.

She stands distanced from the foot of

my bed wearing a royal blue, low cut,

tight sweater and a tight black skirt.

Her dyed red hair is teased.

Her
expression
is causing
lines of
tension on
her face.
She stays
for a short,

uncomfortable visit and leaves.

My stomach is churning.

The next day, the nurse brings me

"Mommy's" matzah brei and I eat.

When I become a young adult, I make

matzah brei for myself and binge on it

regularly. It's not like Mommy's.

I could never again have Mommy's matzah brei, no matter how I try to make it.

ELLEN

I'm in the hospital for what feels like forever.

I'm in a double room.

They wheel in Ellen.

She's my new roommate.

Ellen has cerebral palsy on all of her body and has the use of only one limb, her left arm.

She can't walk, either.

Ellen and I talk and talk.

We laugh often.

We play games from our beds.

We dream together about walking.

We see a TV program called "This is

Your Life" on which a woman walks

again, after a long time of being an

invalid.

We decide that we, too, will walk again.

Ellen leaves Brooklyn Jewish Hospital

long before I do.

Her parents tell me that I brought Ellen

out of a depression.

I didn't know what a depression was.

But I figured it meant that she had been

sad.

She didn't act sad with me.

We were laughing much of the time.

We had fun together.

I was glad that they appreciated me and liked me.

LUCIANO

Luciano comes into my room every day to empty the garbage and sweep the floor.

Luciano appears to have three elbows on his left arm.

His skeleton has points and bends in unusual places, with his slim stature bent over to one side.

Luciano is kind to me each day and I'm kind to him.

I remember his sweetness always.

I look at Luciano and I prefer my own

challenges to having the challenge of

looking like he does.

Looking back, I imagine he looked at

me, a 10 year old, lying in a body cast

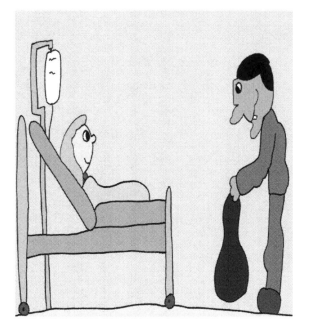

for so many months,

with no family visitors, and he probably would not have wanted to change places with me either.

GOD

A s a little girl, as far back as I can remember, I beg something out there to help me understand.

Before life in the hospital, the sky was

black and empty.

No one to love me, to hold me, to

comfort me.

Except this huge Light that I feel in my

life.

The Light that I talk to each day, often

each hour, more often, each minute.

The Light becomes my best friend.

It becomes my mother and my father.

It becomes a presence I call God.

As I grow up, I talk to God every day

and every night.

I feel Him communicate with me.

Those conversations are the beginning

of a small part of understanding that I

have to be in this house, with these

parents.

I don't have to know why.

I can trust that God does know and that

there is a reason.

As an adult, I look back and wish that I

may have had one person to talk to, one

person to teach me,

one person to look up to.

I don't know why I was not granted

that.

But I believe I found the Almighty very

early because I did not have anything or

anyone else.

It seems that God always provides, in

some way.

We can't really understand the actual

truth behind what happens to us and

the why.

INCREDIBLE . . . DESPITE

It is incredible to me that despite
being treated the way I had been,
I more than survived.
I thrived.

And as a preteen and teen, despite being
surrounded by friends who were
shooting and using drugs,
I never took a recreational drug.

It is incredible to me that despite

spending so much time in the streets, at

night,

I was never attacked.

It is incredible to me that despite having

so many try to take advantage of my

naiveté,

I was still a virgin the first time I got

married.

It is incredible to me that despite not

being lovingly held, encouraged, or

esteemed during the most formative

years,

I am able to love and be loved.

It is incredible that despite being

rejected, beaten, abandoned, and

ignored,

I am a well-adjusted person.

I don't know why I had to live through

those conditions.

But I do know that in some way I was

protected.

And that protection had to be from The

Almighty.

I know always that God is here for me,

that I get help when I call,

and perhaps I get even more help when

I am too weak to call out,

because that means I need the help even

more

WHO IS RIGHT?

I hear God answering me through images and thoughts.

As a 3rd grader walking home from

school, I ask Him often,

"Who is right? You or my mother?"

There was a difference between what I

felt God was telling me to do,

and what my mother told me to do.

GOOD NIGHT TO GOD

God is with me all the time.
He answers me. He tells me lots
and protects me.

I can't relax enough to go to sleep unless
I say good night to God.

So I say a short prayer.

I don't know where I heard it or what it
means.

But I'm sure to say it every night before
bed as a way of saying goodnight to
God.

"Now I lay me down to sleep

I pray the Lord my soul to keep

If I should die before I wake

I pray the Lord my soul to take."

When I grow up and learn how to be a
Jew, I continue to say good night to
God.
I say Goodnight to God by saying the
Shema Prayer.

VISITORS

Jehovah's Witnesses visit me as I lay
in my hospital bed.

They bring me little books that I find
attractive.

The books have pictures and they read
them to me.

They leave some of the books on my bed
to look at when they are not there.

They feel special to me, the books and
the Witnesses.

The books are about relationships and
everyday things in people's lives.

The Witnesses who visit me are very
pleasant.
I like when they come.
They're feeding my keen interest in and
deep hunger for God.
They are very different from Mommy
and Daddy.
They are people I can look up to.

JEWISH

I look back on the time of my
childhood through the lens of one
who is now an Orthodox Jew.

I find it ironic that, at age 10,

I was in Brooklyn Jewish Hospital for a

whole year,

recovering from wounds I had received

from my Jewish parents.

I had been, at the time, ripe and hungry

for being brought to God, and to the

religion into which I was born -
Judaism.

If only even one person had tried to
bring me near.
But the only people to attempt to give
me any religious education,
or any loving words in that place were
not Jews - not a one.

When it was time for me to leave the
hospital,
Miss Kaplan, a Jewish social worker,
working for a Jewish agency, Jewish
Family Service,
placed me in Elizabeth Milbank
Anderson Home for Girls, a Children's
Aid Society Home.

The home practiced Roman
Catholicism.
I heard the rosary every night as the
girls were on their knees at the foot of
their beds.
After some time, I knew it by heart.
I attended church every Sunday . . .
hearing an angry priest scream at us
that the Jews killed Jesus.

But I knew that God loved me and cared
about me
and so always, He was with me,
no matter what religion surrounded me.

In my teen years, I searched and found
Jehovah's Witnesses again.

But being with them did not feel as

"loving" as it had when I was a child in

the hospital.

And so, I lost interest.

THE TRAY

I can't leave the hospital because the osteomyelitis infection is still draining. There is a large hole in my left hip from which the infection drains.

The area is covered with a bandage measuring a square foot, over the draining hole.

A nurse's aide is approaching me carrying my lunch tray.

I'm busy coloring and so the blanket is not covering me.

Rather, it is crunched at the foot of my bed.

I look up to see the aide's eyes rest on

my bandage, which is filled with colors

from draining puss.

I watch her eyes widen as she gasps and

drops the tray.

I'm not aware of how frightening the

colors of puss coming through the

bandage appear to others . . .

Until her reaction.

But to me it's just an awareness.

It does not bother me.

HAPPY & SAFE

I'm happy in the hospital.
I'm getting more love and attention
than I have ever gotten in my life.

I'm safe.

No one is beating me.

No one is hating me.

No one is telling me that I am a horrible,

stupid person.

People are smiling at me.

I'm able to make others feel better.

WHOSE LEGS ARE THESE?

A tall, thin, balding man approaches my bed, holding what looks to me like a machine gun. He calls out my name as he stands by the foot of my bed.

The practice was to call the name to make sure they have the correct patient. Not able to hide, I tell the man that he is at the right bed.

The man explains that he's going to
remove my casts.
I'm frightened.

The man turns on a machine that
sounds more like it will take down a
building than simply remove a body
cast.
He assures me that I won't feel it.
I have no choice but to cooperate,
despite my fear that it will hurt.

The casts are off.
I see my legs for the first time since the
surgery.
My legs are now the same size as my
wrists and forearms, really skinny and
emaciated.

I can't believe those are my legs.

They have no muscles or shape.

My legs look like sticks.

OUT OF BED

Now, I can sit in a wheelchair for a short time each day.

I can finally get out of bed and use the toilet, rather than the bedpan.

During the six months I have spent in this bed, my casts were bonded together with a long bar keeping my legs from moving and separated from each other. In order to change the sheets, several nurses had to hold me up, on my side.

Now I am able to get out of bed in order for them to make the bed.

At the time, I had two wishes, one of which has been answered, that is to be able to go to the bathroom, rather than use a bedpan.

The other was to be able to run around the block.

IF ONLY . . .

The knowledge that they wanted to amputate my leg at the hip gives me nightmares and fears for years to come.

The fear of losing my leg stays with me for a long time.

I believe in my heart that if only I could walk, nothing else would ever bother me.

If only I could walk, I would be happy forever.

I could not imagine that anything else could ever upset me or bother me.

If only I could walk . . .

THERE'S NO SUCH THING . . .

The Physical Therapist teaches me
to use crutches.
It's very difficult for me.

After not using my legs for so long, they
lack muscles.
I have to bear all of my weight on my
right leg.
I work hard learning to use crutches.

I master walking in the hospital hallways.

One morning, the PT takes me down the hospital hallway to a heavy grey door. She opens it.

I see a cold, grey, heavy looking
stairway in front of me.

The PT demonstrates holding both
crutches on her right side, one vertically
and the other horizontally, as she holds
the banister with her left hand.

She shows me how she lifts herself up a
step in that stance.

My turn . . .
I try.
My leg buckles.
My butt lands on the step. I sit there.
"I can't!" I tell her.

She sits down on the step next to me.

She lifts my face level with hers and

looks at me, eye to eye.

"There's no such thing as can't!" she

tells me.

"There's no such thing as can't." she

repeats.

I listen. I hear her.

Her words resonate with my soul.

I never forget.

I repeat her words to myself over and

over, then, and throughout my life . . .

"There's no such thing as can't."

This PT changed my life.

She changed the shape of my fate.

And I don't even remember her name.

May her soul be uplifted for the hope

and the possibilities which she opened

me up to throughout my life.

RUN, NOT WALK . . .

If there's no such thing as can't, then I
won't walk.

I will run.

Every time I hear someone say anything

that means that I won't be able to ever

walk again,

I think to myself that they're right.

I won't walk.

I will run!

THE COMPLAINER

I'm moved into the hospital Children's Ward.

Instead of a hospital room with just two beds, as I had been in, there are more than ten beds here.

The girls in the Children's Ward talk with me.

I make friends with Kim, whose bed is on the other side of the ward.

We like talking with each other and we
have fun, even though we are mostly
stuck in our beds.

Audrey is in the bed next to mine.
Audrey, blond and medium build, is
here for a head injury that she got
falling down the stairs at home.
Audrey is getting on my nerves because
she complains and moans all day, and
all night.
It's hard to sleep with all her moaning.

Kim and I are both annoyed with
Audrey.
We have staff people help us build a
clothesline contraption with string and a

handmade box that allows us to send

private messages back and forth to each

other.

We draw pictures of Audrey that

express our annoyance and anger at her.

We are really into criticizing her,

together.

One afternoon, I overhear Audrey's

mother talking to a visitor.

She tells her that Audrey's skull was

broken by the fall and that it's very

painful.

I hear Audrey's mom say that it can't be

fixed.

Then I begin to understand that Audrey

will likely die very soon . . .

Now I can't believe how cruel I have been.

I feel totally guilty for being so annoyed at her.

I learn very early the bad feeling of speaking negatively about a person, the bad feeling of judging another unfavorably.

My regret is great.

I vow to never again hurt anyone like that.

For the rest of my life, I try to stick to my vow.

CHANGE OF DIRECTION

Now I'm able to be in my wheelchair for more time each day.

I visit the babies on this floor of the hospital and I play with them.

I visit other kids who are new here.

Living in the hospital, I'm happier than I have ever been. Before being in the hospital, my behavior was heading in a troubled direction.

Living at home, I chose friends who intentionally broke the rules and I joined them.

Before living in the hospital, I lived with the harrowing knowledge that I was not wanted. My mother often told me that I was an "accident," whatever that meant, and that she tried to get rid of me even when I was in her womb.

She described using a sharp tool in her effort to do away with me.

I felt deprived of being loved.

NO INFLUENCE

There was no wise influence.
No one to influence or direct me.

No one to tell me any way
to be, any laws in life that
I may follow, any wisdom.

No one to care what I did, or if I did.

No one but The Light.
Without that there was total darkness.

WITHOUT A MOTHER'S LOVE

M y whole life I wonder, I ask
God, "How could you give me
a mother who does not love me?"
A mother who is not a mother?
Who ever heard of such a thing?
It defies the whole definition of what a
mother is.

I cannot even fathom what that would
do to a person to know that their mother
does not care for them, or about them.
Yet, it is what happened to me.

It is what I lived with and continued to
live with.

I watched movies that showed scenes of
mothers who loved and did everything
to be with their child.
The message I took from those movies is
that a mother's love is the one thing in
life that cannot be damaged or taken
away.
Everyone's mother loves them.
Nevertheless, I never had that.
How can anyone understand?
How can I?

And so I ask God and I don't get a real
answer other than that He watches over
me and is there for me.

And He is.

And it is my own relationship, as I
learned and experienced the Holy, Ever-
presence of something that gives me
strength and high spirit, the Light I feel
that sparks joy inside me, that makes me
dance like no one else, even on crutches,
that makes me able to run endlessly,
and appear as if I am flying.

It is as if in my mother's efforts to
destroy me, she did not notice the spirit
that radiated within me no matter what
she did to me and no matter what she
deprived me of.

4ᵀᴴ GRADE BANDIT

A s a 4th grader, to make up for those feelings of deprivation, I go to the candy store on the corner across the street from PS 98 and I take all of the comic books from the rack.

I am trying to make up for what I did not receive at home by taking something else for free.

I also go to a toy store where I take

paper dolls from the shelf, which we

called cutouts.

I get caught by the couple who own the

store. Somehow, they don't call the

police.

Their kindness and understanding make

a huge impression on me.

I never steal anything again.

THE BLESSING OF OSTEOMYELITIS (AND OF LIVING IN BROOKLYN JEWISH HOSPITAL)

Years later, in college, I read studies in which hospital patients' lives changed when they were put in a sterile environment, such as a hospital.

I look back and realize that is what God did for me.

Is it possible that osteomyelitis,

requiring a year in the hospital, could be

a kindness from God?

Was it His way of getting me out of the

hateful house?

The hospital is, for me, an environment

free of the bad influences, free of the

beatings, free of the hate and rejection.

No one here rejects me. They all give me

love - the nurses, the doctors, the other

patients.

I'm truly happy living in Brooklyn

Jewish Hospital.

I compare it to my life before, where I

was the kicking post, the punching bag,

a piece of dirt.

I was a little girl in the house living with

Mean Mommy and Bad Daddy.

Nothing made sense. I tried to be good.

If I was good or bad, it didn't make a

difference in how I was treated.

No one noticed what I did, either way.

They noticed me only to hit me and to

show me hate.

I got attention when they wanted to

express their frustration with each other,

and with life.

I tried to protect myself by curling my

body into the shape of a ball on the

floor, curling my body against the wall.

But the kicks and belts still landed on

my body.

The feeling of my father's shoe landing

on my face was so familiar that it was

almost nostalgic . . .

Nostalgic in that I preferred it to the

abandonment.

I preferred that to the times of no one

even noticing me.

Moreover, the physical pain drowned

out the pain of the emptiness inside of

me, the pain of being despised by the

very people who are supposed to love

me, simply because I'm their daughter

and they are my parents.

The blows to my body distracted me

from the fact that I didn't receive love,

love that I desperately needed.

It was easier to cope with the physical

damage than with the emotional agony.

In Brooklyn Jewish Hospital, none of

that exists.

Here and now, I am loved . . . and I am

safe.

BAD NEWS

After a year of living in the hospital, Miss Kaplan, the social worker, is sitting in a chair near my bed explaining to me that I will have to live in a home where other girls live.
She's telling me that I have to leave the hospital.

My stomach is churning. My nerves and my heart are hanging on the ceiling.

When it becomes night, the ward is
dark.

I go to sit in the bathroom, where there
is a light on.

I try to distract myself by looking at the
pictures in comic books.

I'm terrified of leaving the hospital.

I talk to God all night.

I don't want to leave.

I'm happy here. I'm safe here.

Why do I have to leave?

I stay up all night. It's futile to even try
to sleep.

There's nothing I can do.

They won't let me stay here.

I understand.

But I'm miserable.

THE NEW HOME

I am driven to Elizabeth Milbank Anderson Home for Girls, (I find out years later it is a Children's Aid Society Home.)

As I am driven up, I see a wooden building surrounded by a wooden outdoor porch in the country.

I am directed to go in the door on the side of the building.

Up the steps on my crutches, I enter a

large, cold looking dining room.

There's a huge metal pot on the stove.

It gives me an awful feeling.

The next morning they're making hot

cereal in the pot.

I can't eat.

I'm taken to a large, lower level room

where a heavy-set, tall, masculine

looking woman asks me my size.

I don't know.

She guesses correctly and gives me a set

of clothes: shorts, a tea shirt, underwear,

and socks.

Those are my clothes for the week.

Next week a new set is delivered to my
bed, cleaned and folded.

I'm taken to the ward where my bed is
one of about 15 beds.

I'm given a corner bed near a window.

The grounds are pretty. I'm the only
white girl in the dorm.

That is comfortable for me.

Miss Harris and most of the nurses in
the hospital were black . . .

And I loved them . . .

And I wished they had been my mother.

THE NURSE

I'm taken to the nurse, Miss Mallon. (I don't remember her real name.) She explains to me what happened to my hip and tells me very strongly that I'm not to put any weight on my hip and what would happen if I do.

Miss Mallon checks on me often and I heed her instructions about not putting any weight on my left side.

THE HOUSEMOTHER

In the dorm, the girls talk about things that I'm not used to hearing. I learn all kinds of sexual ideas and words.

There is much plotting against the heavy-set housemother whom they hate. She sits in front of the door to the ward all day and stares at the girls.

They complain that she takes their food
and candy.

In turn, the girls pour talcum powder on
the stairs to make them slippery, in
order that the housemother would fall.

Instead, I, not knowing what they did,
fall down the stairs as my crutch slips
on the powder.

THE INFIRMARY

I get rushed to Dr. Levine and then,
when I'm sent back to the home,
I spend a few days in the infirmary.
I like it better there than in the dorm.
There is a beautiful younger girl in one
of the beds singing "Jesus loves me, yes
I know, for the Bible tells me so . . ."
I hear the tune many times after that.
I remember the tune throughout my
adulthood.

CHURCH ON SUNDAYS

We go to church every Sunday.
We are driven there in the back
of an open truck.
The ride is special to me.
It reminds me of a hayride in the
country.

But the service is unsettling to me.
The atmosphere is cold.
No one talks to me there.
Sitting on one of the hard cold benches,
I see the preacher's face turn red as his

screams that the Jews killed Jesus get louder and louder.

I know I'm a Jew, even though I don't know what it means.

I know the preacher has a lot of hate.

I don't like being in the church.

MY NEW DORM

My dorm is changed to a different group.

They're all taking Spanish and I don't
understand what they're saying.
In my first half-hour there, several of
them are screaming at each other, a
violent kind of screaming, until one of
them, in her rage, slams through a glass
door.
Glass shatters everywhere. There is
silence. Emergency help arrives to take
her to the hospital.

SO UNHAPPY

I cry to Miss Mallon daily that I'm so unhappy here and that the girls are

not doing nice things. She calls me a "sweet prude" as she checks my health and my hip.

DEAR MOM . . .

I send letters to my mother to please take me home. Don't make me stay here. I hate it so much. I'm so uncomfortable here.

I write her, begging, that I want to go home.

 My mother answers.

She writes that it's better for me to live here.

LONELY AGAIN

I go to the grass area behind the building often.

I talk to God from there.

I get close with some of the girls.

I tell them about God and how to talk with Him.

They listen to me. It's helping them.

Until one of the older girls tells the others that I'm having something she called hallucinations.

In other words she told them that my
talking with God means that I'm crazy.

They all stop talking to me.
I'm lonely again.

RUN

I want to run.
I visualize myself running on clear green fields.

I can feel in my mind's eye, the full stretch of my legs as I run smoothly and freely under the bright sun.

I see myself running.

I feel myself running in my body, every day.

Wash-time in the morning takes place in an institutional type bathroom with sinks lined up down the center of the bathroom.

Toilet stalls are situated against the walls, at a right angle to the sinks. My wheelchair fits right under one of the sinks. I'm about to wash my face and brush my teeth.

I turn on the hot water faucet.

The pipe leaks and hot water drips onto

my thigh.

It's scalding hot.

I leap out of my wheelchair.

I run to the other side of the bathroom.

A dead silence comes over the

bathroom.

I look around.

The girls are all staring at me . . .

Their mouths hung open.

I don't even realize the significance of

what has just happened, until I see all of

them stopped cold in their places.

I RUN.

I ran.

The leaky water was so hot that I got up
and RAN.

I did it.

I kept saying to myself for years that I
will not walk.

I will run.

And here it happens.

I run.

But this is not how I pictured my
miraculous recovery – running from a
sink in the bathroom.

It's supposed to be on the fields under
the sun with the glory of God shining on
me.

God has answered my pleas.

I can see, in my mind's eye, the physical
therapist telling me:

"There's no such thing as can't."

I'm brought, on my crutches, to Miss
Mallon.

She seems very reserved about my
runing.

I think she cares about me. But she is
frightened for me. She is wary of my
putting weight on the leg that she had
warned me would collapse if I ever did
that.

She advises me not to put weight on
that leg again, until I see the doctor.

THE DOCTOR VISIT

D r. Levine sits on the high stool as
he speaks with me.
He asks me to try to walk, but to do that
using my crutches.

I don't understand his instructions.
So I take my crutches under my arms,
and lift the tips into the air as I walk.
Dr. Levine's eyes are noticeably teary.
He calls in his staff to see me walk.

Even the people in the waiting room
come over to where I'm walking.
Everyone looks so happy.

Dr. Levine says that I'm walking
without a limp.
He reminds me that in the first surgery,
he had removed 1/3 of my leg because
of the lack of circulation (necrosis.)
And my legs, at this time, are the same
length.
I don't limp at all.
He said it's a miracle.

Then, we go into his office where he is
sitting behind a desk.

He warns me to never do the three
following activities: ball playing, skiing,
or skating.
I leave the office thinking, "There is no
such thing as can't."

Back in the dorm, I don't want to be
there.
My crutches sit at the wall next to my
bed, abandoned.
I love the feel of my legs on the solid
ground.
I walk with the largest strides possible
for me.

I walk wherever my legs take me.
There is sparse supervision in the home.

I walk outside the grounds of the home,

onto a road.

Eventually, I notice a park and go on the

pathway that leads to the entrance.

Two boys, one of them holding a

basketball, enter the park as I do.

I stand on the sideline watching them

play basketball.

I ask them to show me how to play.

And they do.

I continue to play after that.

At a follow-up appointment with Dr.

Levine, he looks at my legs.

His voice cracks. His face looks stunned.

"What have you been doing?" he asks

me.

I don't understand why he looks at me
like that, until he comments on the
defined muscle development in my legs.

I admit to him that I play ball regularly
(even though he had warned me not to.)
But he doesn't even argue with me.
He gives me his blessings to do
whatever sport I choose.

When I am in high school, he gives his
okay for me to participate on the high
school basketball team.
And years after that, to play basketball
for Brooklyn College.

TEENAGER

TAKEN BACK

My mother drives up to the home
and takes me to where she is

now living

She lives in an apartment in Arverne

Housing Project in Far Rockaway.

It's a few blocks from the beach.

Terrible things happen in that

apartment.

Probably because she hates me so

and even more because she hates
herself.

I get much solace from sitting on the
jetty in the midst of the ocean, watching
and hearing the waves, as I talk to God.

I attend Far Rockaway High School.

When we go to the school building
office for the first time to register me,
the school administrator sees that I had
not attended school since 5th grade.

They tell my mother that I will be
placed in a fifth grade class. I am now 15
years old.

My mother seems to understand better
than I do the harm that would bring me

sitting as a 15-year-old in a fifth grade classroom.

She tells me to leave the office and wait outside.

When she is done, I hear that I am placed in a 9th grade class. Looking back, I appreciate her advocating for me.

But I am not able to do the work at all, even though, socially it is more appropriate and the best alternative at the time.

In the summer I am a mother's helper in the morning and then work in the hospital later in the day. I love working with children.

THE LIGHT FROM THE
HALLWAY

I have my own tiny bedroom at the
end of the hallway.
The door opens as I sleep.
The hallway light shining into my room
awakens me.
I squint my eyes in the glare to see a
stranger, a man, standing over me at the
side of my bed.

My mother is trying to introduce us and seems to want me to be with him. He has dark balding hair, and is not clean-shaven.

As I am waking up, I see him turning away, recoiling from my bedroom. I watch my mother follow him out of my room as she pleads with him to stay.

A different night, I am again awakened

to see, yet, another man with my mother

in my bedroom.

None of the men ever touch me.

They do not seem to want to.

I believe the Almighty protected me

from permanent harm.

No matter what anyone intended to do,

I believe, that God made them turn

away from doing anything to me.

I do not have protective parents.

But I do have a protective God.

MY SHAME FOLLOWS ME

Shame is a product of going through the life I was put into.

It is shame that has prevented me from putting what happened into words until now.

And shame still prevents me from writing even more of what happened.

Huge shame that began within me, with my mother.

I am so ashamed.

I am so ashamed that my mother came

onto strange men in front of me, even as

a little girl.

She did it. But I feel the shame.

I am so ashamed that she came onto my

friends when I was a teen.

I am so ashamed that during all those

years, I was such a nothing that not

even a mother could love me.

How horrible I must be.

Everyone's mother loves them. By some

freak of nature, mine never did.

I am so ashamed that I had been such an

outcast.

That I was ignorant, stupid, simple-
minded, unable to focus enough to learn
anything academic.

I am so ashamed of feeling that my
ugliness compares to that of a piece of
dirt whom everyone steps on with no
thought.

Ashamed that I spent so many years not

being fed . . .

and then so many years not being able

to stop eating . . .

and so many years not wanting to hold

my food in needing to throw it up, as if

food was love and the love I was taking
in was sour.

I am so ashamed that I have needs, and
more ashamed that I have unmet needs.
I am ashamed when I want to be
someone's friend who seems to have no
interest in me.
So ashamed that I need connection.
Ashamed that getting my human needs
met was so frustrating and not
happening.

I had been ashamed that I felt large, for
my breasts were so huge, and I was of
tall stature.
I would have preferred to be tiny, to be
short, in essence to be invisible.

I am ashamed that I stand out no matter
how I have tried to hide.

I am ashamed of not fitting in, no matter
where I go, that I do not belong
anywhere, or to anyone.
Ashamed that no one has my back, for
that further proves I am unworthy.

I am so ashamed of trying with all my
might to accomplish a task, to read a
page, to pass a test, to find my way,
with no one rooting for me, no one
caring whether I succeed or fail,
whether I come home at night, or
whether I live or die.
It's shameful to be so disregarded.

It's just plain embarrassing to be so unwanted.

But I must wonder if all this shame was really the foundation of my understanding myself and others.

Was shame the origin of my non-judging ability to listen and to really hear? Did my non-judging begin with the feeling that I am not better than anyone and so would not even think of judging another?

Is my shame the nucleus of my clarity of vision and the root of my ability and desire to care for another?

I wonder . . does it all begin with the shame that we work so hard to overcome?

A MOTHER'S LOVE

During the year and a half that I live in my mother's apartment,

Veeta is my best friend.

It is almost twilight outside.

I go over to her apartment, which is in

the same housing project.

I walk in the front door .

There I see it!

Veeta's mother is sitting at the kitchen table where she is cuddling Veeta's little redheaded brother in her lap.

I more than see it.

I feel it.

For the first time in my life . . . I feel a mother's love.

It fills my whole mind and body.

It makes me happy.

I leave Veeta's house, ambling in the
evening air, under the stars in the black
sky, dreaming, re-feeling it . . .

The wonderful feeling of a mother's
love.

I know it is not mine for now.

But now I know that it exists;

And for now that is enough.

HOSPITAL KITCHEN

I'm 16 ½
My mother kicks me out again.

This time she does not leave.

Instead, she drives me to a room in an
attic in Brooklyn, where I am to pay for
my rent.

And then she stops all communication
with me.

I continue my job in Peninsula General
Hospital kitchen in Far Rockaway. I bike
there.

My job is to prepare meals by putting
the menu items that the hospital
patients had ordered onto the moving
belt.

Then, after the patients eat what is on
their trays, I go to the floors and collect
the trays from their rooms.

I like that part because I get to smile at
the patients and they smile back.
Then I take the trays down to the
kitchen and "strip" them.
That part is disgusting.

Sometimes I would find sets of dentures on the tray and had to find out whose teeth they were.

In the summer there are other high school girls working there.

But during the winter, it is a lonely job for me because all of the other kitchen workers are from Jamaica and I'm not able to understand their English.

So there is no one to talk to there to break the boredom.

To cope, I go into the huge kitchen refrigerator and eat the coconut cheese pie, the whole pie.

CALENDAR GIRL

After paying the rent for the attic room, there does not seem to be enough money left for other expenses. I bike everywhere so carfare is not an issue. But I have to pay for my books, food, and all of those other expenses that just come up.

Veeta and I hang out in Washington Square Park in Greenwich Village, NYC.

We make a few close friends, and Veeta
finds a boyfriend.

My close friends know I need money.

Veeta's boyfriend tries to help by
suggesting that I take a job with a man
he knows.

He recommends me.

The job is posing for a calendar.

He sets up a meeting for me with the
man to take place in a room in a flat.

I show up and so does the man.

He looks me over.

I know I had been good calendar
material at the time, unable to find a bra
large enough to hold in the full vastness
of my chest.

The man talked with me for a while.

He told me about the calendar he was

creating.

I cooperated with whatever he wanted.

Then . . .

"You are a nice girl." He told me.

"Someday, you will have a husband and

you will have a job.

If your husband or your boss sees you

on this calendar, you will lose your

husband and you will lose your job."

"I don't care." I tell him. "I need the

money."

The man stands up, walking away. He lifts a wad of money out of his back pocket and throws the money at me.

The man walks to the door and leaves the building.

At the time I don't understand the ramifications of posing for that kind of calendar.

But God does and He saves me.

God seems to always leave me no choices in things that I do not understand.

It's as if He made my choices for me until I was ready to make my own.

Now, as an adult, 99% of my decisions are from me.

But still I know that when I ask for help in making a decision, or help in anything, I get it, even if it is not immediate; I know it will be there.

I am like a spoiled child who gets help all the time.

It is the Light From the Darkness.

GROWING UP

CHALLENGES

There were lots of challenges to overcome.

My mom took me back only to kick me out when she was marrying her second husband, Bob.

She told me she did not want me around.

She found a room in the attic of a house
in Brooklyn for me and then cut
communication with me.
I missed her.
I couldn't understand why she didn't
want anything to do with me. It hurt so
much.

ANY MOTHER

I wanted my mother . . . I wanted "a" mother.

Really anyone, any old lady off the street, would have been fine . . .

Better than the knowledge that there was not one person who cared.

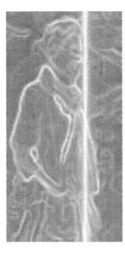 Oh, how I wanted a
mother.
My mother was alive.
She did not die. But
she did not want to be
my mother.

I was orphaned, not by
a death, but by a choice, my mother's
choice to not be my mother, even
though she had given birth to me.

I envied people who lost a mother
through a death.
That parent did not choose to leave and
that child always knows that.
Yet, my mother, even during this
writing, remains alive.

I wonder if others can really understand
or truly empathize that I do not now,
and never had, a mother.

No comforting memories to draw upon
in difficult times.
No words of wisdom to have taken in.

I had only the Almighty, nothing else,
no one else.
The Almighty became my mother and
father.
The Almighty became my Light from
the Darkness.

I felt that way even as I attended
college.

I felt that a oneness, especially, when I
had my first two babies.

After my daughter, Dawn, my second
child, was born, I called my mother to
tell her.
She hung up on me, screaming on top of
her lungs
"You always give me bad news!"

I had no clue how my having two
children could be "bad news" and to
this day just attribute her behavior to
her own illness and distortion.
I attribute her despise of me to
something I could just never
understand.

I am not one to hold a grudge and had

she come to talk to me at any time, now

or in the past, my arms would have

been open.

Who am I that I won't forgive?

ALL PEOPLE WANT TO BE
GOOD

I imagine that each person with whom I interacted has a logical, meaningful explanation for what s/he was doing.

I believe that all people want to be good
and that we each do our best.
I don't hold anger at any of them.

I do feel sad for them, that this was the only way they could deal with their frustrations.

I can't imagine the pain my parents must have experienced to treat their only daughter with such hatred and brutality. And the pain that my mother must have felt her whole life to disconnect from her daughter so completely that at age 95 (2015) when she passed, she continued to despise me.

I imagine their souls will have to come back to try again to do it right, just as I imagine that my own soul will have to do things over, as well.

I believe that there was a reason that the
Almighty wanted me to go through
each of these things.
I choose to find Light in each one.
I choose to make each horror the source
of my life-lessons.
I choose to make them the source of my
Light From the Darkness.

"Had I not sat in darkness,
God would not have been a
light for me."
Midrash Socher Tov,
Tehillim 5

EPILOGUE

GRATEFUL:

A DIFFERENT PERSPECTIVE ON

MY LIFE

Looking back on my life, I ask myself, to whom am I most grateful for the greatest lessons?

I do not get the answer I had expected, just as I did not have the life I had expected.

To whom do I feel the greatest gratitude

for the greatest lessons?

The list is as follows:

I am most grateful to my mean mother

for leaving me no choice but to become

an independent person,

forcing me to find my own resources in

order to survive,

and ultimately to find my closest

confidante and rescuer, The Almighty.

Next, I would have to thank my hateful

father,

who did not have words to speak with

me,

only assaults upon me.

He forced me to learn to be present,

and at the same time to escape my body,

so that I may learn to protect myself

from further assaults.

He caused me to develop my intuition,

so that I may know who may be a

source of harm.

I thank the people who attacked me,

with words, with gossip, with schemes

and with assaults,

for they caused me to develop an inner

strength that, had I not needed it to fight

them off, would never have been

developed.

I thank the family into which I was born

for the loneliness in which I dwelled,

which forced me to learn how to dream,

how to devise ways to avoid boredom,

and to contemplate what might be

possible,

thoughts that kept me sane.

I thank the people who made me fear

them,

for it is through them that I learned not

to fear.

I thank those who cheated me

for through them I learned to be smart

in my business affairs.

I thank the high school teacher who

believed my lie that I cannot do any

more sit-ups

(for I was so bored with them).

She then gave the Phys-Ed-Student-of-
the-Year award to the student who
completed those sit-ups,
but who was not as able as I had been.
I thank her for the lesson that
everything is important, even doing as
many sit-ups as one is capable of.

I thank each child I bore.
I thank each child for teaching me
that children are not the way I think
they are supposed to be.

I thank the child who taught me to love,
not despite limitations but even because
of them.

I thank the child who taught me

that he will not be the way I think he

should be.

Rather, he will turn out his way,

Which, I now understand, is better than

I could have done had he followed what

I had wanted.

Along with that is the lesson that I learn

more from not getting my way than

from having it.

It is from each of my children that I

learned that life is not predictable,

that how people and events turn out is

very different from what I could

possibly imagine.

But the growth I get from that is also
more than I could have aspired for
without it.

I thank the Superior Court judge who
overturned my winning verdict
and caused me to lose what I was
awarded.
It was through her that I realized
that my happiness did not depend on
what I was awarded
or on what I already had.

I thank those on whom I depended for
guidance and support
for not always being so dependable,
for it is through their not showing up
for me

that I cultivated greater wisdom and
inner strength.

I thank each person who challenged me,
my beliefs, my way of thinking,
for each has brought me closer to my
true self.

I thank those who are part of my stories,
those who provided me with issues for
which there were no answers,
but who provided me with the
opportunity to ask more questions.

I thank the Almighty for the infirmity I
have been granted,
for that has led me to enhanced abilities
and greater strengths,

Strengths that I could not have tapped
into, had I not become ill,
Strengths that have led me to being of
more and more service to people about
whom I care.

No, I would not have expected to feel
gratitude for any of these people and
things.
Yet, contrary to what I would expect,
the times that I cried out, begging God
for help
were really the times that He responded
with gifts even better than those I had
requested.

Even though I know there will be more
to endure,

and even though I wish it would be

easier,

I am grateful that much of what I have

suffered

has turned into Light,

and into so many Life-Lessons.

I have learned that my relationship with

the Almighty

cannot not stop the loss, the pain, the

shocks, even the horror.

But it does soothe the suffering.

It does give every event meaning

from which I may gain wisdom

and more appreciation.

Each experience before me,

has blessed me with greater

understanding of how God works

and greater awareness that He does.

I see that I have been gifted with

opportunities to find my own truth and

to be a better version of myself.

It is through these things that in the end,

I find myself most grateful.

May we be open to realize the blessings

in the suffering.

May we not need such suffering to

acquire our Life-Lessons.

May we recognize the good that we

experience as being good.

OPPORTUNITY

I know I'm not the only one. I know that there are so many of us who didn't have a mother or who didn't have a father and those who didn't feel like they had any parent even if it looked to others like they did.

But I believe that we were born to the parents we were supposed to be born to. We were born to those people in order

that we follow our soul's path, in order
that we learn the Life-Lessons we were
put into this world to learn.

We were given to these parents in order
that we have the opportunity to build
the strengths of who we inherently are
and to guide us to be who we can be.

Had I had a loving mother, and maybe
even a loving father, I would not have
had the opportunities to overcome and
build myself, the opportunities to create
myself into who I am today.

The pain with which I struggled forced
me to search and to find answers that
ended up building my character .

In addition, had I not been in such

darkness, I would never have known

what to say to a child who has belt

buckle scar marks all over her back and

legs from the parent who repeatedly

beat her, or to the teen who complains

his mother hates him, or to the adult

who cries that there is no one to reach

out to.

Had I not experienced the darkness that

I did, how could I know what to do with

my darkness and that of others?

Each of our horrors is a disguise for an

opportunity, an opportunity to rise

above and be who we are capable of
growing into.

That is the Light From the Darkness;
that each terrible happening is a
doorway into more insight, more
understanding and into the opportunity
to make the choice to achieve greatness.

We can't hide from darkness.
We can't disregard it.
Darkness gets darker when we try to
resist it.

The dark times present us with a choice.
We may choose to rise above it or we
may choose to drown in that darkness.

Each of us chooses how we want to view our individual darkness.

The darkness can be the source of our greatest Light once we face it head on.

The Light From the Darkness is the opportunity for each one of us to shine.

That is the Light FROM the Darkness.

THE STORY CONTINUES . . .

This book began as a way to put my Life-Lessons stories into a book entitled <u>Light From the Darkness</u>.

But before writing about the Light, I felt I had to bear witness that I had darkness. How can I write about light from darkness if I didn't experience darkness?

So I began to write some of the darkness I had experienced as an introduction to the stories. That introduction became the book you just read.

The stories that I had written and continued to write became the next two books that are soon to be published: <u>Life Lessons Stories of Light From the Darkness</u> and then <u>More Life Lessons Stories of Light From the Darkness</u>. And so the story is continued there.

There you will read stories of my many journeys to create light from the darkness that continued to fill my life. Some of the issues addressed in my journey are my struggles to learn, despite my undiagnosed ADHD and severe dyslexia, which stay with me throughout my life.

Part of that was my inability to learn to read until I was a senior in high school. You will find out how I learned, not only to read, but I learned how to learn. You will read how learning became my life passion.

I did not learn about ADHD until I was 55 years old. I wondered then if my inability to hold onto a grudge was because of my ADHD in that my mind goes right to the next thing. Perhaps because I couldn't focus long enough on one event to be upset about it or even to

remember what the person did until
they did it again. Perhaps that was a
light from the darkness, staving off
what could have been huge anger.
But I had to overcome that in order to
protect myself.

I did overcome.
I overcame huge challenges.
The journey to overcome the obsession
to overeat began after that.

After my mother kicked me out at age
16, I discovered food.
I gained 80 pounds in one year.
You will read about my struggles with
food addiction and how I overcame that

so effectively that food is no longer a problem issue in my life.

You will read about my challenges with illness and disability, and what I learned about real healing. Read how as an older adult, I went from using crutches for the past 20-years to walking again, and to giving my beloved crutches to charity.

You will read also about my near death experience, while I suffered from cancer, and the deep insights and abilities I was gifted from that.

You will also read stories of my challenges in the workplace, how I loved my work but experienced many threats from the system and the personalities, and my journey to overcome them.

You will read about my challenges in overcoming myself, in so many ways, the greatest challenge of all.

Join me on my spiritual journey through various religions. There, I search for and find meaning in those situations that were so difficult for me. I wind up with what gives me true meaning and endless understanding in the faith that I had been born into.

You will read about the recent death of my mother and the understandings and the release that gave me.

You will read about one challenge after another through my eyes and through my evolving perspective.

Join me in Life Lessons Stories of Light From The Darkness. Be with me in my journey to being okay with my life as it is, no matter what, a journey in which I find over and over again, and more deeply, that the key to real joy is to face the darkness, for that is the place of growth, and the place to find the Light.

I hope that my journey helps you, the reader, in some way, and that you glean your own Life-Lessons from mine.

I hope my books help you, the reader, to find your own Light From the Darkness.

ABOUT CHANA KLEIN

Chana Klein, MSEd, PCC, EEM-AP, MCAC, ACG, PACG, CCUG, EFT, NET, AGI, SSS®

Chana writes in the language of stories. Chana shares, through her stories, how she has used the darkness that enveloped her to extract great light and to develop a life-career of helping others to extract their own light from whatever darkness envelopes them.

Chana is a licensed teacher, an alternative medicine practitioner and a life-coach holding more certifications than most people on the planet. She relishes each experience of being there for another person in her many roles, as healer, coach, teacher, mentor, friend, mother, grandmother, writer, and storyteller.

Years of searching for her truth, led to Chana's journey through many religions of the world. Her studies led her to the wisdom of the Torah. She has been studying that wisdom since 1982 for 1 to 6 hours each day.

Chana's wisdom from many areas of study and experience is integrated into her stories.

Chana would love to hear from you:

chana@lightfromthedarkness.com

Chana's websites:

https://lightfromthedarkness.com

http://thespectrumcoach.com

https://theadhdcoach.com

Your review of this book on Amazon would be appreciated.

32419403R00165

Made in the USA
Middletown, DE
03 June 2016